HARRY
at the Beach

written by Ruby Nelson

Illustrated by Danny Noonan

The views and opinions expressed in this book are solely those of the author and do not reflect the views or opinions of the author.

Harry at the Beach - Copyright © 2024 Ruby Nelson

ISBN: 978-1-922664-81-5 (Paperback) 978-1-922664-82-2 (Hardback)
All rights reserved. Neither this book nor any parts within it may be sold or reproduced in any format by any electronic or mechanical means, including information storage and retrieval systems without permission in writing from the author. The only exception is by a reviewer, who may quote short excerpts in a review.

One sunny morning, Harry and Teddy were bouncing with excitement. Today was no ordinary day, it was a beach day! Daddy had already packed the car and Mommy was gathering the last few things.

"Grab your bucket and spade Harry. We're off to the beach!" yelled Daddy.

Harry ran to the door, holding Teddy tight. "We're ready!" he said with a big smile.

But before they could leave, Mommy stopped them. "Not so fast, Harry. We need to put on sunscreen!"

Harry groaned. "I want to get to the beach", but Mommy reminded him, "The sun can hurt your skin if you're not careful." Harry applied his sunscreen and made sure Teddy had his on too.

Once everyone was ready, they piled into the car. Harry and Teddy loved car rides, especially when they sang silly songs about the beach.

Harry wound down his window and the warm air tickled his nose. This was going to be fun. A day to swim and play in the sun!

🎵 Sand in our toes, sun on our nose,
Off to the beach we go!

Seagulls squawk and make a fuss,
Seaweed stinks—it's gross on us!

Rockpools sparkle, shells to find,
Sandcastles tall with moats designed.

The waves go splash, they soak our feet,
The sun is warm and we love the heat. 🎵

When they arrived, the beach stretched out before them. The waves were sparkling like diamonds and glittered with the beautiful sun. The lifeguards were in their tower, keeping an eye out to ensure all the swimmers were safe.

Harry and Teddy jumped out of the car and in a flash, started running down toward the foreshore.

"Hold on, you two! Stay close so we can all stay safe," yelled Daddy.

Harry sighed but nodded. He knew Daddy's rules were important.

Rule # 1. "Always stay where we can see you." Daddy said, pointing to a safe spot near the shore.

Rule #2. "Never enter the water without telling Mommy and Daddy. We need to keep a close eye on you. The ocean is fun, but it can be dangerous too!"

Rule #3. "Always swim between the beach flags set up by the lifeguards." Daddy added, "The guards will keep you safe from strong currents in the water."

Harry and Teddy spent the morning digging deep holes and building the biggest sandcastle they had ever made.

It had windows, a big door and they made little flags from some blue paper they found in the sand. It was spectacular!

"Shoo!" Mommy said as the seagulls arrived. One was cheeky enough to try and grab her sandwich out of the picnic basket.

"These seagulls are hungry," Daddy said with a laugh. "Let's take a walk and see what we can find at the rock pools."

Daddy lifted Harry high into the air, making him feel like a bird soaring over the sand.
"Do it again Daddy, do it again!" screamed Harry as he floated into the sky with teddy.

They walked along the beautiful and warm sand, letting the little waves wash up to their toes.

They stopped at the rock pools, where Daddy explained the rules: "We can look, but we don't touch. We don't want to disturb the creatures who live here."

Harry leaned close to a pool and spotted a beautiful white-and-black shell. Inside, a tiny creature peeked out then darted back in. "Wow!" Harry whispered.

After their walk, it was time for a swim. The water was cool, the waves were gentle, and everyone laughed as they splashed around. Teddy even got a little wet, though Harry made sure to keep him safe.

As the day ended, they packed up their things and said goodbye to the beach. Harry took one last look at the sandcastles they had built, now standing proudly in the golden glow of the setting sun.

They walked back to their car and packed up the umbrella, beach towels, picnic basket and Daddy's surfboard.

On the drive home, Harry cuddled Teddy and thought of the colorful shells he'd found, the sound of the waves and the beautiful sandcastle he'd made.

"That was the best day ever," Harry whispered sleepily.

The day at the beach had been wonderful, but it had made Harry and Teddy very tired! As they snuggled under the covers, Harry dreamed of waves, sandcastles and colorful shells. Teddy, tucked by his side, was ready for their next big adventure—whenever it might come. The day at the beach had been so much fun!

HARRY'S
Book Series

Available Via all Major Online Bookstores

www.ingramcontent.com/pod-product-compliance
Lightning Source LLC
LaVergne TN
LVHW070219080526
838202LV00067B/6853